Apple Power Booster

85g/3oz/¾ cup rocket (arugula) leaves
1 handful watercress
1 apple, quartered
1 stick celery, with its leaves

1 Feed the rocket (arugula) and watercress through a juicer, followed by the apple and celery.

2 Pour into glasses and serve.

Garlicky Apple Power: Omit the rocket and watercress, use 2 apples, and add 1 clove of peeled garlic.

Spinach Power Booster: Use spinach in place of the rocket.

Watercress is rich in antioxidants, which can help prevent cancer and some other diseases. Watercress is also a good source of vitamins A and C.

body-soothing king

Passionate Mango Smoothie

2 passion fruits
1 mango, stoned and peeled
125ml/4floz/½ cup low-fat natural (plain) yogurt
225/8floz/1 cup skimmed milk
Few ice cubes

1 Scoop the flesh and seeds out of the passion fruits and feed through a juicer with the mango.

2 Place the passion fruit and mango juice in a blender, along with the remaining ingredients, and blend until smooth.

3 Pour into a glass and serve.

Spiced Coffee Granita

450ml/15floz/2 cups strong black coffee
4–6 tbsp demerara sugar (light
  brown sugar)
Grated zest of 1 orange
Pinch ground cloves
Pinch ground cinnamon
Pinch ground nutmeg
4 tbsp double (heavy) cream (optional)

1 Stir the sugar, most of the orange zest, and the spices into the freshly made black coffee and let cool.

2 Pour into a shallow freezer container and freeze for 2–4 hours until slushy.

3 Scoop into a blender, add the cream, and whiz to break up the ice crystals.

4 Serve immediately, with the reserved orange zest sprinkled on top.

Irish Coffee Granita: Add 2–3 tbsp Irish whiskey to the blender.

Brandied Coffee Granita: Add 2–3 tbsp brandy to the blender.

Pomegranate and Apple Juice

2 pomegranates
Few fresh mint leaves
4 crisp apples, quartered

1 Cut the pomegranates in half and scoop out the seeds.

2 Feed the seeds through a juicer, followed by the mint leaves and finally the apple.

Passion Fruit and Apple Juice:
Replace the pomegranate with
4 passion fruits.

Powerful antioxidants in the pomegranate may help prevent cancer and prevent hardening of the arteries. The seeds are an excellent source of fibre.

Berry Crush

Three or four 85g/3oz/¾ cup portions of:
  strawberries, blackberries, raspberries,
  blueberries, loganberries, bilberries,
  or cherries, pitted
125ml/4floz/½ cup orange or apple juice
1–2 scoops orange or lemon sorbet

1 Place your choice of fruit in a
  blender with the orange or apple
  juice and blend until smooth.

2 Pour into glasses and add a
  scoop of sorbet.

Creamy Berry Crush: Use scoops
of raspberry ripple ice cream in
place of the sorbet.

Green Goddess Smoothie

4 kiwi fruits, peeled and cut into wedges
115g/4oz/¾ cup gooseberries, trimmed
2–3 tbsp caster (superfine) sugar
  or clear honey
225ml/8floz/1 cup of milk or Greek-style
  natural (whole-milk plain) yogurt

1 Reserve a few slices of kiwi fruit to
decorate. Place all the ingredients in a
blender and blend until smooth.

2 Pour into glasses and float the reserved
kiwi slices on top.

**Dairy-Free Gooseberry and Kiwi Fool
Smoothie:** Proceed as above, replacing
the milk or yogurt with either soy milk or
soy yogurt.

The fruit filled with immune-boosting nutrients and milk or
yogurt loaded with calcium make this
a great health-boosting drink.

Pineapple is a good source for vitamin C and **bromelain**, which can help heal to wounds.

Summer Surprise

½ melon, seeded, peeled, and cut into chunks
½ pineapple, peeled and cut into chunks
1 mango, stoned and cut into chunks
115g/4oz/1 cup blueberries
1 tsp Klamath blue green algae (optional)

1 Place all the ingredients in a blender and blend until smooth.

2 Pour into glasses filled with plenty of ice.

Berry Surprise: Replace the blueberries, with strawberries, raspberries, or other berries of your choice.

Apricot and Prune Stand-By

6 pitted prunes, chopped
400g/14oz can apricots, in their juice

1 Place the ingredients in a blender and blend until smooth.

2 Serve over ice.

Peach and Prune Stand-By: Replace the canned apricots with canned peaches.

Pear and Prune Stand-By: Use canned pears instead of the apricots.

Prunes are an **appetite suppressant**, so they are a perfect start to the day if you are watching the scales.

kung fu bad bacteria

Prune, Apple, and Pear Juice

12 prunes, pitted
2 apples, quartered
2 pears, quartered

1 Place the prunes in a heatproof bowl and cover with 125ml/4floz/½ cup boiling water. Let stand for 20 minutes.

2 Feed the apples through a juicer, followed by the soaked prunes and soaking water and then the pears.

3 Chill before serving.

Apricot, Apple, and Pear Juice: Replace the prunes with 8 stoned dried apricots.

Tomato Treat

8 medium tomatoes
Small handful fresh basil leaves
125ml/4floz/½ cup low-fat natural
   (plain) yogurt
115g/4oz/½ cup low-fat cottage cheese
1 tsp brewer's yeast, optional
2 sticks celery to serve

1 Place the tomatoes, basil, yogurt, cottage cheese, and brewer's yeast in a blender and blend until smooth.

2 Pour into glasses and serve with the celery sticks to stir.

Spicy Tomato Treat: Add ½ of a seeded red chilli for a little extra zing.

Salad Treat: Add ¼ of a cucumber, cut into chunks.

This low-calorie smoothie has **brewer's yeast,** a valuable vegetarian source for the B vitamins, iron, and zinc – all vital for a well-balanced diet.

Blackberry Delight

1 banana, peeled
115g/4oz/1 cup blackberries
175ml/6floz/¾ cup apple juice

1 Reserve 1 or 2 blackberries and 1 or 2 slices of banana to decorate. Place all the ingredients in a blender and blend until smooth.

2 Pour into tall glasses and decorate with the reserved fruit.

Raspberry Delight: Replace the blackberries with raspberries.

Raspberry and Orange Delight: Replace the blackberries with raspberries and use orange juice instead of the apple juice.

Basil and Orange Juice

4 oranges, peeled and segmented
Small handful basil leaves
Orange slice and basil leaves to serve

1 Feed half the oranges through a juicer, then add the basil leaves, followed by the remaining orange segments.

2 Pour into a glass and decorate with the orange slice and basil leaves.

Tomato and Basil Juice: Instead of the oranges, use 4 large or 6 medium ripe tomatoes. Feed half the tomatoes through the juicer, then add the basil, followed by the remaining tomatoes.

Orange and Parsley Juice: Use parsley in place of the basil.

Tomato and Parsley Juice: Use tomatoes and parsley and proceed as for Tomato and Basil Juice.

The beneficial volatile oils found in basil have antibacterial properties and can provide anti-inflammatory benefits. Basil is also a good source of beta carotene.

Citrus fruit such as grapefruit, oranges, lemons, and limes are loaded with vitamin C, which has an antihistaminic effect that can reduce the nasal symptoms associated with a cold.

Citrus Zing

1 grapefruit
3 oranges
1 lemon
1 lime

1 Juice the fruit: either cut in half and use a citrus juicer, or peel the fruit and feed the segments through a juicer.

2 Serve immediately for the maximum dose of Vitamin C.

Apple and Citrus Zing: If using a juicer, feed 2 crisp apples through the juicer after the citrus fruit.

Cherry and Orange Juice

Large handful of cherries, pitted
3 oranges, peeled and segmented

1 Feed the cherries through a juicer, followed by the orange segments.

2 Pour into a glass and serve.

Cherry and Orange Smoothie: Blend the cherries in a blender until smooth. Squeeze the oranges, add the juice to the blender, and whiz again.

It has been suggested that cherries have painkilling properties. One thing is for certain – they are packed with pectin, a fibre that can help lower cholesterol, and they are a good source of vitamin C.

love your life

Pineapple Energizer

1 pineapple, peeled, tough core
   removed, and cut into chunks
1 peach, stoned and cut into wedges
115g/4oz/1 cup strawberries, washed
   and hulled
Few blackcurrants
Freshly squeezed orange juice

1 Place the pineapple, strawberries, and
currants in a blender with 125ml/4floz/
½ cup of orange juice; blend until smooth.

2 Add more orange juice to thin to your
desired consistency and serve.

Blue Pineapple Energizer: Use
blueberries in place of the blackcurrants.

Carrots are rich in beta
carotene and are good for
the immune system, skin, and
eyes. Cardamom is thought to
help fight colds and fever.

Creamy Carrot and Cardamom Dream

6 carrots, trimmed
4 tbsp single (light) cream, low-fat
   fromage frais (yogurt), or quark
Seeds of 4 cardamom pods, crushed

1 Feed the carrots through a juicer.

2 Stir in the cream, fromage frais (yogurt),
or quark; add the cardamom seeds.

3 Pour into a glass to serve.

Creamy Carrot and Coriander Dream:
Replace the cardamom with a small
handful of coriander leaves (cilantro) and
feed through the juicer.

Creamy Carrot and Parsley Dream:
Replace the cardamom with a handful of
parsley and feed through the juicer.

Blackberry and Apple Juice

225g/8oz/1¾ cups blackberries
2 apples, cut into wedges

1 Reserve a few blackberries
and slices of apple for
decoration. Feed
the blackberries
and apples through
a juicer.

2 Pour into glasses
and decorate with
the reserved fruit.

**Raspberry and Apple
Juice:** Replace the
blackberries with
raspberries.

Cranberries can help prevent or alleviate cystitis and other urinary tract infections. They can also help prevent kidney and bladder stones.

Peachy Cranberry Fizz

115g/4oz/1 cup cranberries
1 tbsp caster (superfine) sugar
2 peaches, stoned
225ml/8floz/1 cup freshly squeezed orange juice
Clear honey or maple syrup, if desired
Sparkling mineral water to serve

1 Place the cranberries in a small pan with the sugar and 2 tbsp water. Cook for about 5 minutes until soft, then let cool.

2 Cut the peaches into pieces and place in a blender with the cranberries and orange juice. Add a little honey or maple syrup if you want a sweeter drink. Blend until smooth.

3 Strain through a nylon sieve, if desired, to remove the seeds.

4 Pour into glasses and top up with the mineral water.

Nectarine and Cranberry Fizz: Use nectarines in place of the peaches.

Plum and Cranberry Fizz: Use 8–12 plums in place of the peaches.

Raspberry and Banana Tofu Smoothie

115g/4oz/1cup raspberries
1 small banana, peeled
175g/6oz/¾ cup soft tofu
350ml/12floz/1½ cups freshly squeezed
   orange juice

1 Place the raspberries, banana, and tofu in a blender and blend until smooth.

2 Add the orange juice and blend again.

3 Pour into glasses and serve.

Strawberry and Banana Tofu Smoothie: Replace the raspberries witHstrawberries.

Blackberry and Banana Tofu Smoothie: Use blackberries instead of raspberries.

Tofu, a good all-round food, is high in protein, calcium, and vitamin E, and low in saturated fats, making it great for strong muscles and bones.

live life to the full

Fruity Beety Beauty

2 beetroots (beets), trimmed
1 large orange, peeled
Small handful fresh raspberries

1 Cut the beetroots (beets) into quarters and feed half through a juicer.

2 Next feed the orange segments through, then the remaining beetroots (beets). Pour the juice into a blender.

3 Add the raspberries to the blender and blend until smooth.

4 Pour into a glass and serve.

Enjoy this juice to boost your immunity. Beetroot is a good source of folate and vitamin C.

Blueberries are full of **antioxidants**, which may slow down the aging process. Yogurt is a good source of calcium.

Blueberry Yog Nog

115g/4oz/1 cup blueberries
225ml/8floz/1cup low-fat natural
   (plain) yogurt
1 tbsp clear honey
1 tbsp sunflower seeds

1 Place the blueberries, yogurt, and honey iin a blender and blend until smooth.

2 Pour into glasses and sprinkle with the sunflower seeds.

Raspberry Yog Nog: Use raspberries in place of the blueberries.

Yog Nog with Pumpkin Seeds:
Use pumpkin seeds instead of sunflower seeds.

Passion Zoom

1 small mango, peeled, stoned, and
   cut into chunks
1 wedge pineapple, peeled and cut
   into chunks
12fml/4floz/½ cup orange juice
1 passion fruit

1 Place the mango, pineapple, and orange juice in a blender and blend until smooth.

2 Cut the passion fruit in half and scoop out the seeds. Add to the blender and blend briefly.

3 Pour over ice and serve.

Creamy Passion Zoom: Replace the pineapple with a peeled banana.

This refreshing juice is packed full of antioxidants that are perfect for building up your **immune system**.

Nutmeg has **calming** properties and the other spices help to give this drink a warming cosy spiciness. The oats will help to stave off any hunger pangs until morning.

Hot & Spicy Apple Sleepy

2 apples, peeled, cored, and sliced
50g/2oz/¼ cup raisins
2 tbsp rolled oats
¼ tsp each ground cardamom,
   cinnamon, and nutmeg
Extra nutmeg to serve

1 Place the apples, raisins, oats, and 350ml/12floz/1½ cups of water into a small saucepan.

2 Bring to the boil, then reduce the heat and simmer gently for 5 minutes. Stir in the spices.

3 Let cool slightly, then carefully pour into a blender and blend at a low speed until smooth.

4 Pour into heatproof cups and sprinkle a little nutmeg over each drink before serving.

Chilled Spicy Apple Smoothie: Chill the apple smoothie and serve cold.

Hot Choc Froth

350ml/12floz/1½ cups milk
1 tbsp cocoa powder
50g/2oz plain (dark) chocolate, broken
   into chunks
1 tbsp icing (confectioners') sugar
Few mini marshmallows

1 Place the milk in a small pan and heat until almost boiling.

2 Place the cocoa, chocolate, and sugar in a blender and carefully pour in half the hot milk. Blend until smooth.

3 Add the remaining milk and blend until frothy.

4 Pour into two heatproof glasses or mugs and top with marshmallows.

Almond Choc Froth: Add 25g/1oz Amaretti biscuits and ½ tsp almond essence (extract) if desired.

say bye-bye to muscle aches

Rosemary Red

200g/7oz/1½ cups raspberries
115g/4oz/1 cup redcurrants
115g/4oz/1 cup blackcurrants
125ml/4floz/½ cup orange or grape juice
1 tsp freshly chopped rosemary

1 Place all the ingredients in a blender and blend until smooth. If desired push through a nylon sieve to remove seeds.

2 Pour into glasses and serve.

Ginger Red: Add 2.5cm/1 inch piece of peeled and grated ginger root in place of the rosemary.

Tarragon Red: Use tarragon in place of rosemary.

Cold Buster

2 kiwi fruits, peeled and cut into wedges
2 apples, cut into wedges
2 tbsp lemon juice
1 tsp echinacea (optional)

1 Feed the fruit through a juicer.

2 Stir in the lemon juice and echinacea; serve immediately.

Pear Cold Buster: Replace the apples with pears.

Echinacea (available from health food shops) helps relieve the symptoms of colds and flu. The antiseptic properties found in lemon juice are also good for fighting off colds.

Berries are good sources of **proanthocyanins** and vitamin C, which are required for a healthy immune system. They may also have properties that protect against cancer.

Apricot Hormone Juice

225ml/8floz/1 cup soy milk
3 tbsp probiotic yogurt
1tsp tahini
6 apricots, stoned
Few toasted sesame seeds

1 Place the milk, yogurt, tahini, and apricots in a blender and blend until smooth.

2 Pour into glasses, sprinkle the sesame seeds on top, and serve.

Peach Hormone Juice: Use 1 peach in place of the apricots.

This juice is high in calcium and the apricots provide potassium. This drink has a balancing effect that may help when **hormones** are affecting your mood.

The sour flavor of the gooseberries is counteracted by the sweetness of the kiwi fruits in this **immune-boosting** juice, which is a good source of vitamin C, potassium, and bioflavonoids.

Gooseberry and Kiwi Juice

6 kiwi fruits, cut into wedges
150g/5oz/1 cup gooseberries
1 sweet apple, quartered

1 Feed the ingredients through a juicer.

2 Pour into a glass and serve.

Gooseberry, Pear, and Kiwi Juice: Omit the apple and use 4 kiwi fruits and 2 quartered pears.

Red Berry and Willing

115g/4oz/1 cup strawberries, washed and hulled
115g/4oz/1 cup blueberries
1 tsp ginseng powder (optional)
2.5cm/1 inch piece of ginger root, peeled
1 tbsp clear honey
125ml/4floz/½ cup freshly squeezed orange juice

1 Reserve a strawberry and a few blueberries. Place all the ingredients in a blender and blend until smooth.

2 Pour into glasses, decorate with the reserved fruit, and serve.

Currants, Berry, and Willing: Add some redcurrants and blackcurrants for a super fruity smoothie.

Blueberries are a good source of zinc and other nutrients that can give a boost to the reproductive hormones of both men and women. Strawberries have long been thought of as the fruit of love.

Broccoli, carrots, and cucumber are good sources of zinc, which is vital for healthy sperm.

One for the Men

4 carrots, trimmed
85g/3oz/⅓ cup broccoli florets
¼ cucumber, peeled
4 tbsp ground almonds
1 tsp pumpkin seeds
1 tsp sunflower seeds

1 Feed the carrots, broccoli, and cucumber through a juicer.

2 Stir in the ground almonds.

3 Pour into glasses, sprinkle the seeds on top, and serve.

Another for the Men: Replace the broccoli with a handful of watercress.

Make a Date with Sleep Smoothie

1 banana, peeled
115g/4oz/½ cup amazake
4 fresh dates, stoned and chopped
125ml/4floz/½ cup milk or soy milk
Freshly grated nutmeg

1 Place the banana, amazake, and dates in a blender and blend until smooth.

2 Thin with milk or soy milk to your preferred consistency.

3 Sprinkle generously with nutmeg.

Dairy-Free Banana and Date Smoothie: Replace the milk with apple juice for a dairy-free alternative.

Banana and Raisin Smoothie: You can use 2 tbsp of seedless raisins instead of the dates.

Bananas contain the amino acid tryptophan, which helps you sleep, and nutmeg has phytochemicals, which also aid sleep.

Sleep Easy

1 tbsp fine oatmeal
80ml/2⅗floz/⅓ cup boiling water
90g/3½oz/1¾ cups iceberg lettuce
2 sticks celery
2 carrots

1 Place the oatmeal in a blender and pour the boiling water it. Let cool.

2 Feed the remaining ingredients through a juicer and stir into the oatmeal mixture.

Tomtato Sleep Easy: Replace the carrots with 1 large tomato.

Making Simple Juices

Some recipes for smoothies require the addition of fruit juices. You can use shop-bought juices, but if you have a juicer, you may want to make your own fresh juice for your smoothies, or you may simply want to make single fruit juices to drink. Here is a guide to how much juice you will get from the most popular fruit and vegetables.

To make 225ml/8floz/1 cup you will need:

Apple Juice: 4–5 apples
Orange Juice: 3–4 oranges
Pineapple Juice: ½ medium --pineapple
Tomato Juice: 4–6 medium tomatoes
Carrot Juice: 5–6 large carrots
Grapefruit Juice: 2 grapefruit
Grape Juice: 225–300g/8–10oz/
  2–2½ cups grapes
Mango Juice: 1½–2 mangoes
Pear Juice: 4–5 pears
Cherry Juice: 450–500g/1lb–1lb2oz/
  2–2½ cups cherries
Pomegranate Juice: 4–5 pomegranates

Use these quantities only as a guide. These juices were made using a centrifugal juicer (see pages 16–17). If you use a masticating juicer, you will get a larger quantity of juice because these machines are more efficient. Also remember that the amount of juice will vary between the different varieties of the same fruit and even from season to season. Ripe local fruits in season are usually juicier than fruits that have been picked unripe and flown across the world.

Juices Hints and Tips

Recipes make one to two glasses, depending on the size of your glass and the amount you want to drink. In general, vegetable juices are drunk in smaller quantities than fruit juices.

Stick to one type of measuring system. Never switch between them. Cup measurements are for standard American cups.

Always use fruit and vegetables that are in peak condition.

Wash fruit and vegetables well before use.

Prepare fruit and vegetables just before you need them. Some vitamins will start to be destroyed when you cut into the produce, and some fruit and vegetables discolor quickly.

Use organic ingredients if you want to avoid pesticide residues.

Cut vegetables into pieces that can be fed through the juicer's feeding tube easily. This will vary from machine to machine. Some machines will take whole apples, others will need the fruit or vegetables to be cut up in small pieces.

Insert soft fruit such as strawberries and blueberries slowly to extract the most juice. Follow soft fruit and leaves with a harder fruit such as an apple or a vegetable.

If you do need to store the juice, keep it in the refrigerator and add a few drops of lemon juice. (This will keep it from discoloring.)

Serve well chilled – use chilled vegetables and fruit or serve over ice.

Dilute juices for children with an equal quantity of water. You can use sparkling mineral water to create a fizzy fruit drink.

Fruit is high in fructose, a natural sugar, so people with diabetes should not drink too much. Dilute with water if necessary.

Do not drink more than 3 glasses of juice a day unless you are used to it – too much juice can cause an upset stomach.

Very dark vegetables such as beetroot (beet) and broccoli can have strong flavors. Dilute with water or with a milder flavored juice such as apple or celery if you want.

Smoothie Bases

Many smoothies are 100 percent fruit, but to blend efficiently a liquid is often added.

Fruit juice:
In 100 percent fruit smoothies, fruit juice is added if necessary. If you have a juicer, juice your own fruit to maximize the vitamin content (see pages 12–13). For speed or convenience, you can use shop-brought juices. Chilled juices not made from concentrate have the best flavor.

Yogurt:
When yogurt is added as a base it adds valuable calcium to the smoothie. Using a yogurt with live bacteria is good for the digestion, providing healthy bacteria. Greek-style yogurt will give the creamiest results but has the highest calorie content. Whole-milk yogurt can be used as a substitute for Greek-style yogurt. It adds more creaminess to the drink than a low-fat yogurt, with a calorie content that is higher than low-fat yogurt but not as high as Greek-style yogurt. Fruit-flavored yogurt may have a lot of added sugar.

Milk:
Like yogurt, milk added to smoothies provides a good source of calcium. Calcium is important for growing children, and smoothies are a good way of including milk in a fussy child's diet. Whole-fat milk has the most flavor, but for those wishing to reduce fat content, skimmed or semi-skimmed milk is better.

Cream:
For special occasions, adding single (light) or double (heavy) cream to a smoothie will give it a richer flavor.

Crème fraîche, fromage frais, quark, cottage cheese, mascarpone:
These dairy products can be added to smoothies to provide calcium and as thickeners. The fat content varies and those with a high-fat content such as full-fat crème fraîche and mascarpone should be used in moderation. Low-fat crème fraîche, cottage cheese, and fromage frais can be used more frequently. Cottage cheese and other low-fat cheeses also add protein and make a smoothie more filling. They are good additions when a smoothie is being served in place of a full meal.

Ice Cream and sorbet:
These can be added to smoothies for extra creaminess or flavor, as well as to to cool the drink. They can be blended with the fruit or added by the scoop in place of ice.

Dairy substitutes:
Tofu is high in protein and low in fat. It is a good source of calcium and contains vitamin E. It has little flavor but will give your drink a more satisfying thickness and creamy texture.

Soy milk and soy yogurt can also be used as an alternative to dairy products, as can rice milk and oat milk. You can also use coconut milk, banana, and avocado to give smoothies a creamy texture and good flavor.

Smoothie Hints and Tips

Recipes make one to two glasses, depending on the size of your glass and the amount you want to drink.

Stick to one type of measuring system. Never switch between them. Cup measurements are for standard American cups.

Wash fruit and vegetables well. Peel if required and cut into chunks.

Use fruit and vegetables in peak condition.

Prepare fruit and vegetables just before you need them. Some vitamins start to be destroyed as you cut into the produce, and some produce discolors quickly.

Add liquids such as fruit juice, milk, or yogurt to the blender first.

For maximum nutritional benefit, serve the drinks immediately after preparing them.

Smoothies may separate on standing. This does not affect the flavor. Serve with a straw twizzler or spoon to stir before drinking.

Fresh ripe fruit should provide enough natural sweetness, but you can add a little extra sugar or honey to sweeten if required.

Keep berries and chopped up soft fruit such as apricots, peaches, and bananas in the freezer to make instant iced smoothies. They can go into the blender when frozen.

Smoothies are best served cold. Chill the ingredients before use and serve with plenty of ice. Crushed ice will cool a drink quickly. You can also use ice cream or sorbet.

Smoothies tend to be thick, but you can alter the thickness of the drink to your taste. Simply add extra milk, water, or fruit juice to achieve your preferred thickness.

If the smoothie is too thin, add a banana, which is a great thickener, or some frozen ingredients such as frozen fruit or ice cream. Or use cooked rice to thicken the smoothie.

You can remove seeds, pips, or fibrous material from the smoothie by straining through a nylon sieve. This will remove the fibre content, thus affecting the nutritional value of the drink, but it is useful if you find them unpleasant or you have fussy children.

Some liquids increase in volume and froth on blending so never overfill the blender.

Make sure the lid is firmly on your blender before processing.

Wash the blender as soon as possible after use. If fruit becomes dried on, soak in warm soapy water for a few minutes to soften the fruit.

Equipment

Whether you want to make juices, smoothies, or both, there is certain equipment that will be essential to have in your kitchen.

Juices

If you want to make juice from hard fruit and vegetables such as carrots, apples, and pears, you will need to invest in a juicer. There are two main types of juicers available.

Centrifugal juicer: This is the least expensive type and it works by finely grating the fruit or vegetables and then spinning them at high speed to separate the juice from the pulp, which is then discarded.

Masticating juicer: This machine is more efficient, but it comes with a higher price tag. It finely chops the fruit, then forces the juice out through a fine mesh.

Food processor: Some types have a centrifugal juicer attachment. It will not be as efficient as a dedicated machine; however, it will be more than adequate for occasional juicing.

Citrus juicer: Citrus juicer attachments are available for some juicers and food processors. These are specifically designed to squeeze juice from citrus fruit and are the most efficient equipment for juicing this kind of fruit. However, you can squeeze citrus fruit by simply peeling and feeding the segments through the juicers. Alternatively, you may prefer to use a simple hand lemon squeezer or reamer.